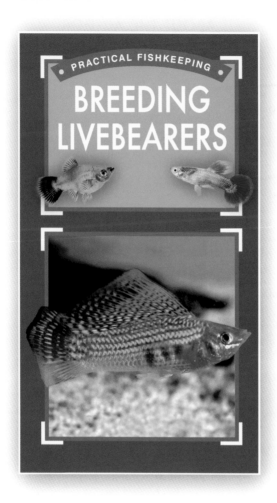

PRACTICAL FISHKEEPING

BREEDING
LIVEBEARERS

John Rundle

RINGPRESS

ABOUT THE AUTHOR

John Rundle, a former marine engineer, now devotes himself to breeding fish – a hobby he has enjoyed for more than 35 years.
John is a regular contributor to *Practical Fishkeeping* magazine, and is a well-respected lecturer. He works part-time for the University of Plymouth, where he runs a breeding programme for cuttlefish based at the Marine Biological Association of the UK.

SCIENTIFIC CONSULTANT: Dr. Peter Burgess BSc, MSc, MPhil, PhD is an experienced aquarium hobbyist and international consultant on ornamental fish.

Commercial products shown in this book are for illustrative purposes only and are not necessarily endorsed by the author.

Photography: John Rundle (pages 10, 11, 26, 27, 36, 38, 40, 43, 46 – bottom, 55, 58), Peter Burgess (pages 34, 35, 38, 51, 53, 57 – bottom, 64), Peter Gathercole (page 46 – top), Keith Allison, D.J. Wilby (page 13 – bottom), and courtesy of Tetra UK, Interpet, and Practical Fishkeeping Magazine.
Line drawings: Viv Rainsbury
Picture editor: Claire Horton-Bussey
Design: Rob Benson

Published by Ringpress Books,
a division of Interpet Publishing,
Vincent Lane, Dorking, Surrey, RH4 3YX, UK
Tel: 01306 873822   Fax: 01306 876712
email: sales@interpet.co.uk
First published 2002

ISBN 1 86054 271 9

Printed and bound in Hong Kong through
Printworks International Ltd.

10 9 8 7 6 5 4 3 2 1

CONTENTS

INTRODUCTION

Like many fishkeepers, I was won over to breeding tropical fish when I saw a guppy give birth to young fish in my community tank. This instant one-tank breeding success soon became apparently flawed – and posed several problems:

- How to save the newborn fry from being eaten by the parents or other tankmates.
- How to ensure the fry have the correct foods for a good rate of growth.
- How to produce good-quality fish.

This book will help you to overcome these problems, and covers practical methods of breeding the popular fancy aquarium livebearing fish, such as the guppy, swordtail, platy and molly.

Many newcomers to fishkeeping think these colourful man-made varieties that are seen in aquarium shops are easy to breed. There are two direct answers to this point – yes and no.

Yes, these fish will readily produce young fish, even in the confines of the living-room community tank; but no, it is not easy to produce *quality* progeny using ad-hoc breeding regimes.

All the fancy-coloured, finned livebearers seen in aquarium shops are produced by very stringent selective

Although some fish will readily breed in an aquarium, good results cannot be guaranteed. An organised breeding programme is essential. Pictured: Blue Platy.

breeding programmes, mostly by commercial fish breeders.

In such a small book it would be impossible to cover all the aspects of what can be an intense subject, and that can require the use of detailed genetic study. This book will, however, supply enough information on how to keep and produce healthy, good-quality, fancy livebearers by using basic selective breeding methods.

CHAPTER 2

WHAT ARE LIVEBEARERS?

This book covers fish that have been cultivated by fish breeders from the original wild species they come from and the genera *Poecilia* and *Xiphophorus* of the family Poeciliidae.

FAMILY POECILIIDAE

This group contains more than 30 genera and sub genera. Within it there are some very interesting and well-known fish, including those from the genus *Gambusia*.

Gambusia affinis is known as the Mosquito Fish, a common name that is well suited. It originates from the USA, but has been introduced to many parts of the world as a control to eradicate mosquitoes, since the fish feeds on mosquito larvae.

There is another species of livebearer with the same common name of Mosquito Fish – *Heterandria formosa* –that has an interesting feature, its size. When full grown, the males are only 2 cm (^{3}/4 in) and the females are 3 cm (1 ^{1}/4 in).

The *Heterandria formosa* can be found in parts of Florida and Georgia, in the USA. The fish's reproduction method is based on a remarkable process called superfoetation, a condition where the gravid female can carry two or more batches of embryos at different stages of development. This means the female continually produces a few fry, instead of large, distinct broods.

In the family Poeciliidae, there are the genera *Poecilia* and the genus *Xiphophorus,* from which all the species in this book belong.

The family *Poeciliidae* includes the *Poecilia* (including the guppy, above) and *Xiphophorus* (including the swordtail, below) genera.

- **Genus** *Poecilia*: there are more than 20 species in this genus, and it is here that the guppy and the molly are found. From the quite plain wild guppy all the highly-coloured varieties have been developed.

- **Genus** *Xiphophorus*: this genus contains more than 30 species, including all the swordtails and platies. There are some very attractive wild species of swordtails and platies that make good aquarium fish, but they are not often seen in aquarium shops. The fancy cultivated varieties of swordtails and platies originated from these wild ancestorss.

Poecilia and *Xiphophorus* are native to a wide range of habitats in South Eastern USA, Central America and Central South America.

REPRODUCTION

It is not difficult to determine the sexes of the fish covered in this book. At sexual maturity, the males can be distinguished by the modified anal fin called the gonopodium. This consists of an elongate bony structure, and, on the end, there is a hook-like appendage, which connects to the female during copulation (see also page 60).

The gonopodium introduces sperm into the body of the female to fertilise several batches of eggs, which allows the female to give birth to fry at approximately four-week intervals.

With egglaying fish, the males release semen into the water, that then fertilises eggs laid by the females. Livebearing males operate differently – they do not produce fluid semen, but a globe of sperm held together. These globes travel along the gonopodium, which makes contact with the urogenital pore of the female and allows the sperm to enter her.

From one such fertilisation, the female can store sperm, enabling her to produce several broods of fry over a long period of time. The gestation period for the species mentioned ranges from 21 days to 30 days. An average time at the temperatures suggested (see Heating, page 24) would be 25 days.

When the female is carrying a brood of fry, she is said to be 'gravid' and this area becomes very dark and swollen as the young develop.

The fish in this book are classed as ovoviviparous, meaning the eggs form inside the female without her providing any nourishment to the developing young. The embryos are sustained from their yolk sacs; once this is used up, the eggs will 'hatch' inside the female's body. The young are then 'born' and will be seen swimming as fully-formed young fish.

The breeding strategy of the livebearing fish compared to the egglaying fish is interesting. The livebearers have evolved to produce small numbers of young that are advanced and hence have a better chance of survival; the egglayers produce many hundreds or thousands of eggs to compensate for the very low survival rate.

CHAPTER 3

LIVEBEARER SPECIES

Of the many species of livebearing fish, only a very small number have been cultivated by fishkeepers to produce the various colours, fin and body shapes seen in aquarium shops. Through this cultivation process, they have become, without doubt, some of the most popular aquarium tropical fish in the world. The fish in question are the guppy, the swordtail, the platy and the molly.

Guppy Disease spreads rapidly, so check fish carefully before buying.

The guppy has many colour varieties, including the Red Half-Black Neon, pictured.

THE GUPPY

The name 'guppy' derived from Robert John Lechmere Guppy, a British naturalist, who discovered the fish in Trinidad in 1865. At the time, it was thought to be a new species and was given the Latin name *Girardinus guppii* in honour of its collector. It was later realised, however, that this fish had previously been described from specimens collected in Venezuela. Its Latin name is now *Poecilia reticulata* but the common name 'guppy' lives on.

The wild guppy can still be found in Trinidad, and while they are quite attractive fish, they bear little resemblance in colour and shape to the modern fancy man-made varieties. The brilliant-coloured males, often with wide, flowing caudal fins, make the guppy a very popular fish that is found in aquarium tanks all over the world. Of all the fish covered in this book, it is the guppy that requires the most attention when using it for a breeding project.

When bred by serious breeders for showing, guppies are judged to set standards, and it is at these guppy shows that the skills of the breeder can be seen.

The males can grow to 3.5 cm (1 $^3/_8$ in), and the females to 6 cm (2 $^3/_8$ in).

FIN VARIATIONS

There are now many varieties of cultivated guppies
with set fin shapes, such as the:

- Bottom Swordtail
- Double Swordtail
- Deltatail
- Veiltail.

COLOUR TYPES

There are also numerous colour varieties with fancy
names, such as the:

- King Cobra
- Half Black
- Red Half Black
- Copper Tail.

SWORDTAILS

An adult male red swordtail is a sight to behold, with a
body that could be 10 cm/4 in (the females 12 cm/4 $^3/_4$
in), not counting the famous extension to the caudal fin
that gives this fish its common name.

Swordtails are ideal for the community tank, though,
at times, males can be a bit boisterous to each other,
and a lone swordtail can become a rogue fish in a
community tank. To stop this aggression, keep a
minimum of one male and two females.

Found under the name *Xiphophorus hellerii* (Heckel
1848), this fish has an indigenous geographic range
that extends from Honduras through Guatemala up to
Mexico. It has been bred in captivity since 1864, but
the domestic man-made varieties were first introduced
to the hobby in the 1930s.

The adult male red swordtail is an impressive-looking fish.

VARIATIONS

There is quite a large range of colour and fin shapes that have been developed by fish breeders, including:

- Black Swordtails (all black)
- Red Swordtails
- Red Wagtail Swordtails (a red body with black fins)
- Hifin Swordtails (that have very long extensions to their fins).

A Red Wagtail Sword male.

Lacking the gonopodium, the female swordtail (top) is noticeably different to the male (below).

ROLE REVERSAL

Much has been written and debated about the subject of "sex reversal" in livebearing fish, especially swordtails. There are many fishkeepers who swear that their female swordtail has changed into a male, complete with a gonopodium and a caudal extension, and claim that the fish is capable of mating.

To carry out this miraculous change, not only would the external features have to change, but also certain internal organs. For example, the ovaries of the female would have to change into the functional testes of the male. At present, there is no scientific proof that this can happen. The latest school of thought is that these fish are not reversing their sex but are just late developers. That is to say, the male characteristics – the gonopodium and the swordtail extension – do not develop until the fish are larger adults.

Red wagtail platy: a deep red colour, with black fins. This is a *'maculatus'* species.

THE PLATY

The platy can be found in various colours and shapes that have been developed by fish breeders. These domestic strains are attractive and make excellent aquarium fish, and they do not have the boisterous reputation of the swordtail.

The platy originates from the same countries as the swordtail, and the bulk of the man-made varieties come from the following two species (overleaf).

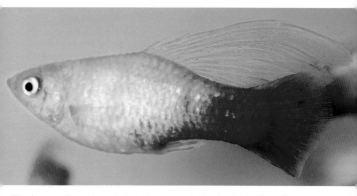

The *'variatus'* species of platy has a more slender body than the *'maculatus'* species, and there are several fin varieties. This is a hifin parrot variatus platy.

- *Xiphophorus maculatus* (males 4 cm/1 $^1/_2$ in) and females 6 cm/2 $^1/_4$ in)). It has a much deeper body than the swordtail and the males lack the extension of the caudal fin.
- *Xiphophorus variatus* (males 5 cm/2 in and females 7 cm/2 $^1/_2$ in). It is commonly known as the 'variegated platy'. The body of these platies are more slender than *X. maculatus*. They were originally yellow/orange fish, but can now be found in many colours and with several fin shapes.

VARIATIONS
- Red Platy (a full red body and fins).
- Blue Platy (the blue body is a reflective metallic colour that can vary according to the lighting conditions).
- Marigold Platy (an orange and light yellow body).
- Moon Platy (a yellow body with a dark half-crescent shape at the base of the tail. The dorsal fin is an orange/yellow).

This is only a few of the many colour varieties developed by fish breeders.

The Marigold Platy has an orange and pale yellow body.

MOLLY COLOURS

The molly comes in a variety of attractive colours, including gold (above) and jet-black (below).

THE MOLLY

Mollies have long been a firm favourite with fishkeepers. In the early years, the only fish found in aquariums were natural wild species. Then fish breeders started to develop the man-made colour varieties that we see today.

It is not hard to see why mollies are such popular aquarium fish – they can have flowing, sail-like dorsal fins, and a variety of attractive colours, including green, gold and even jet-black.

There are three species that have been used to develop these varieties.

- The Giant Sailfin Molly *(Poecilia velifera)* : its natural habitat is Yucatan, Mexico. Males measure 10-15 cm (4-6 in) and females 18 cm (6 ^{1}/$_2$ in). This is a magnificent fish, which has natural colours of sparkling green and gold flecks. It has a large sailfin dorsal that can be 4.5 cm (1 ^{3}/$_4$ in) high.
- The Sailfin Molly *(Poecilia latipinna)* : its natural habitat is South and North Carolina, Texas, Florida and the Atlantic coast of Mexico. Males are 10 cm (4 in) and females 12 cm (4 ^{3}/$_4$ in). This is a beautiful

The green Sailfin Molly is a striking fish, popular with fishkeepers.

The Sailfin Molly's magnificent dorsal fin can stand 3cm high when erect.

fish with a high sailfin dorsal. And is best seen in its natural colours of olive/yellow with bluish flecks. The dorsal fin stretches almost to the full length of the body, and can stand 3 cm (1 ¹/₄ in) high when erect.

- The Short-finned Molly *(Poecilia sphenops):* its natural habitat is in the southern states of America to Venezuela and some Caribbean islands. Males are around 7 cm (2 ³/₄ in) and females 10 cm (4 in). It is easily identified by its short dorsal fin, and its wild colours are generally olive-green with black blotches on the body. It is from these fish that the Black Molly was developed.

The first two species both have the same common name of Sailfin Molly. One method of telling them apart is to count the rays in their sail-like dorsal fins. *P. velifera* has 18-19 dorsal rays, while *P. latipinna* has 14 dorsal rays.

Although often labelled a brackish fish, the molly can thrive in water that does not contain any salt.

WATER CONDITIONS

The molly has often been labelled as a fish that should be kept in brackish water conditions. In fact, it can be kept without any problems in water that does not contain any salt. The only time that a small amount of salt needs to be added is when the water is very soft and acidic.

VARIATIONS

Mollies are now available in a variety of shapes and colours, including red, green, silver, black and marbled.

CHAPTER
4

ESSENTIAL EQUIPMENT

It is possible to obtain all the equipment you need for breeding fish from an aquarium store (although there are a couple of pieces that can be home-made – see pages 22, 30, 31).

FILTRATION
To breed the fish covered in this book, there is no need to spend money on expensive filters. The air-driven filters recommended below are basic but effective.

SPONGE FILTERS
These act as mechanical filters, and have a biological capacity (i.e. they contain bacteria that break down the fish's toxic wastes). They can be bought as a complete unit from aquatic retailers, and come in two sizes: one that will suit the breeding tanks and a larger size that will filter the growing-on or stock tanks.

Sponge filters have many advantages – they are easy to maintain and there is no danger of losing fry that are sucked into the filter.

BOX-TYPE FILTERS
They are small, plastic, box-type internal filters can also be easily found in aquatic retail outlets. Like sponge filters (above), box filters have a mechanical and biological capacity. They can be used to hold various

filter materials, such as synthetic wool and carbon. Being able to use different media or water-softening resins means the fishkeeper can harden or soften the water according to the needs of the fish.

HOME–MADE FILTERS
These very versatile filters can be made to whatever size is required by the fishkeeper – for example, small ones

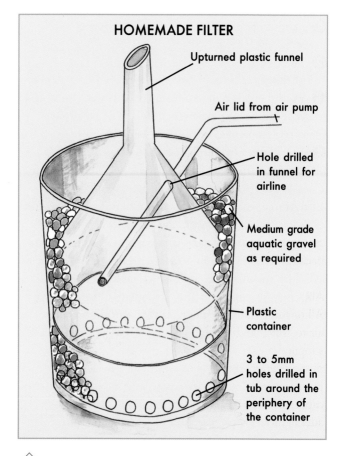

HOMEMADE FILTER

Upturned plastic funnel

Air lid from air pump

Hole drilled in funnel for airline

Medium grade aquatic gravel as required

Plastic container

3 to 5mm holes drilled in tub around the periphery of the container

for breeding tanks, or larger sizes to suit growing-on tanks.

These filters consist of three components:

- A plastic container (square or round ice-cream containers are ideal)
- A plastic funnel
- Aquarium gravel.

❶ Around the base of the plastic container make a series of holes about 3 mm ($^1/8$ in) in diameter.

❷ Then make another hole – the diameter of a normal plastic aquarium airline.

❸ Place enough aquarium gravel in the container to cover the 3 mm holes that should be about 12 to 15 mm ($^1/2$ to $^2/3$ in) up from the base.

❹ Rest the funnel on top of the gravel, and then continue to fill up the container with more gravel.

Every time a water change is carried out, just clean the gravel in the filter in old tank water and replace back in the filter.

AIR

All of these filters require air to work, and this is supplied by an electric air pump. Make sure that the pump has the required capacity to produce an adequate air supply for all the tanks in the project.

The more powerful the airpump, the better. This will ensure that the filters will not be overloaded.

Most air pumps are rated with the output in lph (litres per hour) or the recommended tank capacity in gallons. If unsure, ask the dealer to recommend a model to suit your needs. It would be wise to obtain an air pump that will supply more air than is required; this ensures that you will be able to filter all the tanks and will stop the pump from being overworked.

HEATING

It is well documented that all the fish covered in this book can survive in aquariums that vary in temperature between 18°C (64°F) to 28°C (82°F). A more stable range would be 24°C (75°F) to 27°C (80°F); this is what most tropical community tanks are set at. If any of the fish could be kept and bred at a slightly cooler temperature, then it has to be the guppy (see page 11).

Tank heating can be achieved by using combined heater/thermostats or by heating the air space around the tanks. Space heating is often found in 'fish houses' where a large number of tanks are held. It is usually achieved by using an electric fan heater that has a thermostat control fitted.

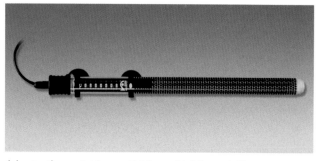

A heater-thermostat is essential for maintaining a stable water temperature.

TANKS

The size of the tanks will be determined by the type of livebearer selected. For instance, an adult guppy measures only 3.5 cm (1 $^3/_8$ in) and an adult green sailfin molly can be up to 15 cm (6 in) in length, so their space requirements will differ. Ranges of average tank sizes that will cover all the fish in this book are in the table below.

LENGTH	DEPTH	WIDTH	FISH TYPE	USE
46 cm (18")	30 cm (12")	30 cm (12")	Guppies or Platies	Breeding tank
61 cm (24")	30 cm (12")	30 cm (12")	Guppies or Platies	Grow-on or stock tank
61 cm (24")	30 cm (12")	30 cm (12")	Swordtails or Mollies	Breeding tank
91 cm (36")	30 cm (12")	30 cm (12")	Swordtails or Mollies	Grow-on or stock tank
122 cm (48")	30 cm (12")	30 cm (12")	Mollies or Swordtails	Grow-on or stock tank

SET-UPS

For a basic breeding project, like the ones covered in this book, there are three set-up systems.
• Stock tanks
• Breeding tanks
• Growing on tanks.

FURNISHED VERSUS BARE TANKS

If breeding livebearing fish in furnished tanks, the set-up should consist of gravel and plants, in fact similar to a community tank. I believe that more control can be gained from using the bare tank set-up – i.e. one that has no substrate (gravel) on the tank base. This arrangement gives the fish breeder control over:

- **Tank cleanliness**
  This is a main factor when breeding fish; a bare tank can be thoroughly cleaned prior to any breeding project. The bare tank method also enables easy removal of debris from the tank floor.

- **Feeding**
  The bare tank is an asset when feeding fish. It allows the amounts of foods being fed to be clearly seen. Live foods and dry foods can, if over fed, lead to pollution and the subsequent death of young fry. The bare tank will allow any uneaten food to be removed with ease by means of a small water change (e.g. using a small-bore siphon tube).

A furnished tank is preferable in an ordinary aquarium, but a sparser set-up is more practical in a breeding tank.
Pictured: a group of platies.

Close observation of your fish is important, particularly when you need to ascertain if a female is pregnant. Pictured: a gravid guppy.

- **Observation**
  The need to clearly observe all the activities in the tanks is a key factor when breeding fish. With livebearers, you will want to see the females that are gravid, observe when the females drop a brood, see early signs of sexual development in the young fish and any characteristics that you are breeding for. The bare tank will allow good observation.

NUMBER OF TANKS NEEDED

This is a difficult point to address, as it will depend on the species of fish (see pages 11, 12, 15, 17). The only generalisation that can be made is that more than two tanks are needed to breed livebearers of some quality.

STOCK TANKS

This is where the intended adult breeding stock fish are held. It is advisable to have the males and females kept apart in separate tanks. If kept together in groups, the control over the mating of individual pairs will be difficult. The selected males or females are held separately, maybe to be crossed back with other fish from the same line.

These tanks can be either a standard planted tank with a gravel substrate, or a bare tank set up that has no gravel substrate.

BREEDING TANKS

In the breeding tank a selected pair is placed together to mate. Then, when the male is removed, the pregnant female is left to drop her brood of young fish. It is based on the bare tank set-up and is where the breeding trap (discussed later) is situated.

GROWING-ON TANKS

Even to make a basic breeding programme viable more than one growing-on tank is needed. These tanks will hold the young fish that are waiting to be sexed; once the sexes of the fish can be distinguished, the males and females are separated and placed in other growing-on tanks. These will be bare tank set-ups similar to bare stock tanks.

BREEDING TRAPS

Breeding traps come in all shapes and sizes, and are either home-made or commercially manufactured (found in aquarium shops). The trap is a unit that can hold the gravid female fish until she produces her brood of young fish, which can pass safely through small openings into the main area of the breeding tank.

The use of breeding traps is another point that is debated by fishkeepers. While it is not a necessity to use traps when breeding livebearers, they do give the fish

TANK SET-UPS

All tanks are shown without covers — the planted tank would have a light in the hood.

A planted stock tank

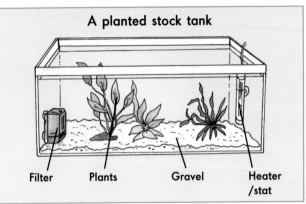

Filter   Plants   Gravel   Heater /stat

A bare stock tank

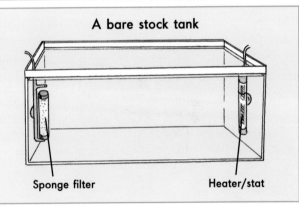

Sponge filter   Heater/stat

A breeding tank

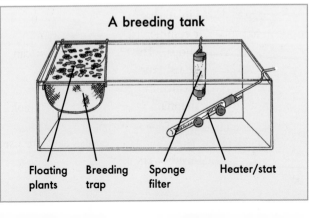

Floating plants   Breeding trap   Sponge filter   Heater/stat

breeder a greater degree of control in terms of the numbers of young fish saved during the first few hours of their life. They help to stop predation by the female.

AQUARIUM SHOP TRAPS

In my opinion, many of the commercial breeding traps are too small. This becomes obvious when they are used to hold large female swordtails or mollies. Pregnant females should not be placed under stress, but this can happen when fish are confined in small breeding traps.

HOME-MADE TRAPS

There have been many versions made and used with good results by fishkeepers, in fact too many to cover

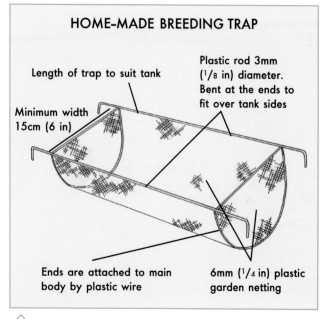

HOME-MADE BREEDING TRAP

Length of trap to suit tank

Plastic rod 3mm (¹/₈ in) diameter. Bent at the ends to fit over tank sides

Minimum width 15cm (6 in)

Ends are attached to main body by plastic wire

6mm (¹/₄ in) plastic garden netting

in this book. One factor that is evident in all the home-made traps is that the fish have a large free-swimming area. This helps greatly to keep the female free from stress – otherwise, a stressed female may abort prematurely.

MAKING WOOL SPAWNING MOPS

❶ Wrap nylon wool around a block of wood around 15 cm (6 in) in length, and cut through with a sharp knife. Tip: to fool the fish into thinking the mops are plants, choose green wool!

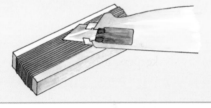

❷ Tie a piece of wool around the middle of the strands.

❸ Create a loop at the top of the strands and then secure the knot. Trim any loose ends where necessary.

The home-made breeding trap suggested in this book is the type I have used to breed livebearers. It is made from plastic garden netting (see sketch) and can be made to suit whatever size of tank required.

Clumps of the Java Moss plant (*Vesicularia dubyana*) or wool spawning mops (page 31) placed in the trap will give cover for the newborn fry while they attempt to leave the trap for the security of the breeding tank.

Wool spawning mops are normally used for breeding egglaying fish, such as tetras. They can be suspended on cork or a strip of polystyrene in the tank, and the livebearer fry can then take cover in between the strands of wool.

LIGHTING

Over-tank lighting is not a necessity to breed these fish if they are kept in bare tanks; normal daylight from a window will be sufficient, but some lighting is necessary.

If there are no windows where you keep your fish, then the electric lights that are used to illuminate the room will supply enough light to breed livebearers. Of course, if tanks that hold stock fish are planted, then the normal tank lighting required to grow plants must be used (see Set-ups, page 29).

A portable light on a wander lead is ideal for examining the young fish in more detail.

PLANTS

While there are many species of tropical aquatic plants that can be used in planted stock tanks, the popular ones used by the author are:

• Indian Fern (*Ceratopterus thalictroides*). This is a true water fern that can be grown submerged or as a floating plant. In its floating form, it provides good cover for young fry to hide in.

- Straight Vallis (*Vallisneria spiralis*). This is used as a tall background plant in stock-holding tanks.
- Java Fern (*Microsorium pteropus*). It grows from a thick rhizome (an underground rootlike stem bearing both roots and shoots) and has young plantlets that form on the main leaves. It is epiphytic, so generally grows attached to wood/rock.
- Java Moss (*Vesicularia dubyana*). It has a mass of branched moss-like stems that makes it the ideal plant to form protective breeding traps for fry.

The last two in the list make ideal plants for bare tanks, providing good cover for fry and also adult fish. Another good point about these two species is that they do well in subdued lighting regimes.

Indian fern (*Ceratopteris thalictroides*).

Java fern (*Microsorium pteropus*).

CHAPTER
5

CARING FOR LIVEBEARERS

This chapter covers what will keep the fish healthy and in good breeding condition. It will also help the fishkeeper to look for health problems when buying stock.

WATER CONDITIONS
The livebearers covered in this book are not demanding when it comes to water conditions; however, there are certain ground rules that should be observed. Water that is neutral to slightly alkaline (7 to 8 pH) and moderately hard (12° to 18° dH) is fine for keeping and breeding them; try and avoid water that is too acidic and soft.

A 25 per cent water change carried out once a week is ideal to maintain the fish in good condition. Beware of large water changes; these fish can react disapprovingly to too much new fresh water. These fish will soon indicate when water conditions in the tank are not right (usually by gasping for air at the surface of the water). This is why small regular water changes are a must.

SALINITY
The question of salinity when keeping livebearing fish has always been a strong point of discussion among fishkeepers. It is frequently written that salt should be used to give the tank water a brackish content; the fact is that there is no actual requirement to add salt to the

Many wild livebearers do not inhabit brackish waters, so salt is not a necessary addition to the aquarium. Pictured: wild guppies (male: left, female: right) from a freshwater stream in Trinidad.

water to keep the fish covered in this book alive and well. Even many of the wild livebearing fish, including the guppy, are mostly found living in fresh waters.

SEX RATIOS

The ratio of males to females within a brood of livebearers is said to be influenced by environmental factors, such as pH and temperature. Basically, the lower range of the pH scale and higher temperatures is said to produce more male livebearers in a brood.

While it is almost certain that these factors can determine the sex ratio in some way, I have found that when breeding guppies at a neutral pH of 7, the broods had more males than females. But, in the same water conditions, other fish, such as killifish and dwarf cichlids, produced more females in the broods.

WATER TEST KITS

It is imperative that these livebearers are kept in good water conditions. To ensure this, it is recommended that the water be tested for pH, ammonia, nitrite, nitrate and hardness. Test kits based on a simple colour change can be obtained from aquarium shops.

Various simple test kits are available for checking your aquarium water parameters.

WATER CHANGES

Large, new water changes can cause health problems, especially to young fish. When carrying out water changes, keep them to around 25 per cent. A twice-weekly 25 per cent water change is far better than a 50 per cent water change once a week.

If moving fish to a tank that has had a complete water change (or new water), ensure that the water in the tank has been left to settle for a couple of days before placing the fish in the tank. The fish will indicate that they are not happy by starting to shimmy and clamping their fins. The key point is to avoid extremes when changing water.

See also Health Problems, page 38.

pH is known to have an influence on the sex outcome of some livebearing fish. At a pH of 7, guppies (above) tend to produce more males than females.

Some guppy breeders feed their fish up to 10 times a day!

FEEDING

It is necessary to feed a good, varied diet to keep the fish in top condition. They will take dry foods and it is possible to feed them totally on a diet of a selection of these foods. However, if live foods and some of the top-quality frozen foods available on the market are added to this diet, the fish will definitely be better for it.

When young, all the fish mentioned in this book benefit from being fed more than once or twice a day. It is not unusual for serious guppy breeders to feed their fish as often as 10 times a day (carefully controlling the amount that is fed each time). By this type of feeding, the fish will develop sexual differences by three weeks of age.

SUITABLE FOODS FOR LIVEBEARERS	
FRY	**YOUNG FISH AND ADULTS**
Live brine shrimp	Live whiteworm
Live microworm	Live grindal worm
Live grindal worm	Dry flake food
Crushed dry flake	Sinking algae wafers
Powdered dry fry foods	Dry freeze-dried *Tubifex* worms

A group of Red-tailed Gold Guppies feeding on an algae wafer.

Of course, the time that you can spare to feed your fish is a factor, but try to feed them at least three times a day. Do not think that one or two big feeds will compensate for three or more smaller feeds. Little and often is the ideal feeding regime.

HEALTH PROBLEMS

Like all types of tropical aquarium fish, fancy livebearers must be kept under good conditions and fed a well-balanced, nutritious diet to keep them healthy. Of course, at times they will have health problems, and they can suffer from the same range of diseases as any other freshwater tropical fish. However, there are certain specific problems that are particularly relevant to this group of fish. It is wise to inspect all fish before buying them from a shop, and new stock should ideally be quarantined for one to four weeks.

MELANOMAS

Melanomas are dark pigmented skin tumours that are fairly common in swordtail x platy crosses; black swordtails are also prone to these tumours. The black colour of the fish can make melanomas difficult to see, but, viewed at an angle, the tumour can be seen as a raised growth. There is no cure, and affected fish should not be bred from.

GUPPY DISEASE

Guppies are prone to what is commonly known as 'Guppy Disease', caused by a tiny protozoan called *Tetrahymena corlissi*. Signs of the disease are small, white patches that consist of large numbers of the parasites clumped together. It can spread rapidly and be fatal. Treat with an anti-protozoa remedy. Heavy infections may not respond to treatments.

White patches on a female guppy. Microscopic examination is necessary to determine whether these are caused by bacteria or ectoparasites.

CAMALLANUS

Small red worms may be seen from the vents of the fish. Contact your vet for a suitable worm treatment.

FURTHER READING

A good fish health reference book when keeping and breeding fancy livebearers is *The A-Z of Tropical Fish Diseases and Health Problems* by Burgess, Bailey and Exell, published by Ringpress Books. Another Ringpress title, *Live Foods for Aquarium Fishes* (in this *Practical Fishkeeping* series) is also recommended reading.

CHAPTER
6

BREEDING METHODS

___

It is again necessary to re-assess the common misconception that livebearers are easy to breed. Yes, they will readily produce young fish, but no, it is not easy to produce quality progeny using ad-hoc breeding methods.

AD-HOC BREEDING METHODS

Fishkeepers will often find baby livebearers hiding in the cover of plants in the community tank, and from that moment they become fish breeders. The problem is, this situation is often the start of ad-hoc breeding methods which are undesirable.

An uncontrolled community tank environment is completely unsuitable for a breeding programme if quality fish are to be produced.

Two of the most common ad-hoc breeding methods stem from keeping livebearers in the community tank:

- The fish are left to mate and the gravid (pregnant) females drop their broods of young in the tank. Other tank inmates will attempt to eat the young fish and those young that miss this fate are left to search for food. This is not a good way to start life; the fry must have the correct type of food and plenty of it. They should not simply be left to forage on left-overs from the larger fishes' menu.

- Another method is where the gravid female is confined in a very small plastic breeding trap that is floating in the community tank. When the female drops the brood, they pass through a grid into a small shallow chamber in the lower section of the trap. This method has many faults: these traps are often too small to hold fish like adult swordtails or mollies. In addition, they are far too small to hold large broods of young fish that could exceed 50 in number. Other disadvantages include the lack of control over growth rates because of incorrect feeding, and the fact that strict breeding programmes cannot be maintained in a one-tank set-up.

BREEDING POINTS

Before looking at a more controlled breeding method, it is worth considering some relevant points about breeding livebearers.

- The fish that you will be working with have probably been part of a strict selective breeding programme – usually by professional fish breeders. This would have been carried out to maintain a special colour, pattern, shape of fins and body, and size.

Swordtails (above) and platies (below) will crossbreed, so breeding stock must be kept separate to preserve purity.

- Some livebearers (such as swordtails and platies) will crossbreed if kept in the same tank. If you want to breed pure red swordtails, and you have a few red wagtail platies in the tank, crossbreeding may jeopardise your breeding project.
- Man-made colour varieties can revert to original wild colours and type if not part of a selective breeding programme. This can happen when breeding guppies.
- Only one factor at a time can be controlled in the breeding project, such as a certain colour, fin shape or even size. It is not possible to capture two of these factors in the same project.
- More than one tank is required.

ACQUIRING BREEDING STOCK

There are three avenues available to obtain the fish that you want to use for breeding.

❶ AQUARIUM SHOP

When you are selecting fish for breeding stock, whatever the type, you should make sure that they are healthy and that all their fins are erect. Select fish that have a good body shape and colour. If asked, many shopkeepers will catch the particular fish you have selected. The species of fish will also determine what factors you look for.

Guppies: one drawback is that when these fish are imported they do not arrive in matched pairs; this makes it difficult to match the exact males to females.

Matching breeding pairs can be difficult, particularly as female guppies are often presented in shops as shoals of mixed colours (as pictured).

The males usually arrive in their individual colour types whereas the females are often in mixed colours. This makes any direct breeding programme difficult, but not impossible, to produce good-quality fish. By selecting males and females that are healthy and have good colour, maybe showing hints of the same colours, a new breeding project can be started.

When selecting the breeding stock, you can either buy a small group of young fish, consisting of males and females, or an adult pair of fish.

Swordtails and platies: these can be found in matching pairs, for example red swordtails, red platies, black swordtails or wagtail platies – these are only a few of the many varieties that are being cultivated by commercial fish breeders. With luck, the individual varieties will be held in separate tanks.

Avoid buying fish that are mixed, for example platies in with swordtails, and even mixed colour varieties in the same tank, as there is a high possibility that these fish will have crossbred. Interbreeding will jeopardise the chance of producing viable individual varieties, causing extra work during a selective breeding project.

**There are many types of platy in numerous colour varieties.
Pictured: Blue Platy.**

Mollies: if individual colour or fin varieties is what is required for breeding projects, then, as with the swordtails and platies (see page 44), avoid selecting fish from dealers' tanks that carry mixed mollies – for example, black mollies with gold mollies.

❷ PRIVATE SOURCE

Try to find a local fishkeeper that specialises in breeding good-quality fancy livebearers, who will sell you 'true' pairs or trios of fish (that is to say that the parentage can be tracked and the fish are the same variety as the one you wish to breed). This is a great advantage when starting a selective breeding programme.

❸ HOME COMMUNTY TANK

Even fish from the community tank can be used in a breeding programme, provided they are good-quality fish. The same points should be observed as with the fish obtained from the aquarium shop. That is, do not use fish that are mixed in the tank, (see above).

AGE FOR BREEDING

It is possible for livebearing fish to mate at a very early age, but this should be avoided at all costs. Very small, young females will produce weak broods that will probably consist of only a few fry.

Another factor is that characteristics, such as colour, fin and body shapes will have not developed sufficiently to allow selection of the best fish for use as breeding stock.

Suggested ages for breeding:
• Guppies: 4 to 5 months.
• Swordtails, platies and mollies: 5 to 6 months.

Swordtails should be at least five months old before they are used for breeding. Pictured: male swordtail *(Xiphophorus helleri).*

BREEDING METHODS

It is necessary to assess in-breeding and line-breeding methods when working with fancy livebearers.

IN-BREEDING

This is the breeding of fish that are closely related. This could be brother to sister, father to daughter, or son to mother.

Carefully done, in-breeding can produce excellent results, as this in-bred guppy shows.

In-breeding has always been a subject of discussion and debate by breeders of cultivated fancy tropical and fancy coldwater fish because of the problems that can arise from this system of breeding.

It is true that, if not controlled, it can be the cause of some degeneration within a variety. It is the breeder's responsibility to use strict selective breeding procedures and to cull deformed fish and runts within a brood.

LINE-BREEDING

Line-breeding is a form of in-breeding, but it consists of running two or more lines of breeding stock. By using two or more females mated with a single male the 'lines' are established. (This is shown in the chart on pages 52-53.) It is quite an efficient way of producing good-quality fancy livebearers, and often used by serious breeders with many tanks that enables them to run several breeding 'lines'.

OUT-CROSSING

There will be occasions when the fish breeder will observe undesirable traits or other defects occurring in an established strain. It could be characteristics such as colour, shape or size.

To correct these problems, the answer may lie in introducing so-called 'new blood' – i.e. out-crossing. This is achieved by crossing fish from the established strain with fish that are distantly related or not related at all.

SELECTING THE BEST

Whatever method you decide to use, the key word is 'selection'. At every step in the breeding programme, select only the best fish and those that show the desirable traits required. Observation is very important. It is possible that you will see some changes (such as body size or fin shape) after several generations. Attention must be paid to these changes, as they can be small or severe.

In-breeding or line-breeding should be stopped if the changes are not what you are looking for. However, if the fish are improving, then the project can be continued.

EXAMPLES OF BREEDING METHODS

IN-BREEDING

❶ Select the best male and female of your breeding stock and house them together to mate. Note that the 'best' fish is not necessarily the largest.

❷ Place the gravid (pregnant) female alone into a tank, which contains the breeding trap.

❸ Remove the female when she produces her brood. Make sure she is not placed back into a tank where other males (those that are not used in the breeding project) are held, as you may wish to use subsequent broods from this female. Also remove the trap. Females need to be rested for 24 hours after dropping their young. Females that have just given birth are more sexually attractive to males so many get pestered more than usual.

❹ Identify the sex of the fish as soon as possible and separate the males from females. If well fed, it is possible to sex the young fish when they are three weeks old.

❺ Take the best male and best female (brother and sister) and put them together to breed.

❻ Go to step 2 and start the cycle again. At times,

IN-BREEDING PROGRAMME

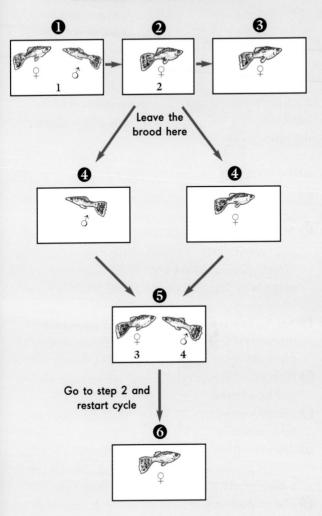

Leave the brood here

Go to step 2 and restart cycle

Key

♂ — Male   ❶ — Step numbers

♀ — Female   1 — Fish number for records

when a high-quality male is found in a brood, he can be bred with close female relations, such as his mother or even his daughter. This tactic can help to improve the in-bred line.

Even after a few years, with careful selection of the breeding pairs, the quality of the fish will not greatly diminish.

LINE-BREEDING

❶ Select the best male fish and place him in a breeding tank with two of his best sisters.

❷ Place each of the gravid females into separate tanks and breeding traps to produce their individual broods. This is the start of two separate 'lines' of fish being bred. For easy identification call them Line A and Line B.

❸ Sex the fish as soon as possible and separate the males from females. Take care to keep the two lines physically apart.

❹ Now take the best brother and sister from each line and breed them.

❺ The procedure should be continued for about five or six generations.

❻ After this time, take the best male from Line A and cross him with a female from Line B, and also cross a male from Line B with a female from Line A.

❼ The breeding procedure carries on like this, with the two lines being kept separate.

Again, with careful selection, these lines can produce quality fish with the colours and traits that the breeder wishes to hold.

KEEPING CONTROL

Observation and record-keeping are important key factors when running systematic selective breeding projects for fancy livebearing fish.

Without the use of careful observation and good written records, a project can soon be destroyed, even to the point of fish such as guppies reverting to the original colours of wild fish.

OBSERVATION

Through all the steps of a breeding project the breeder must observe the fish closely to select the best fish specimens. Deformed fish and those that do not meet the project's requirements in terms of colour, size, or fin and body shape, should be humanely culled.

Without close observation, the desirable traits you are breeding for can be lost. In the case of guppies, they can revert to their wild coloration. Pictured: two male wild-type guppies from Pitch lake, Trinidad.

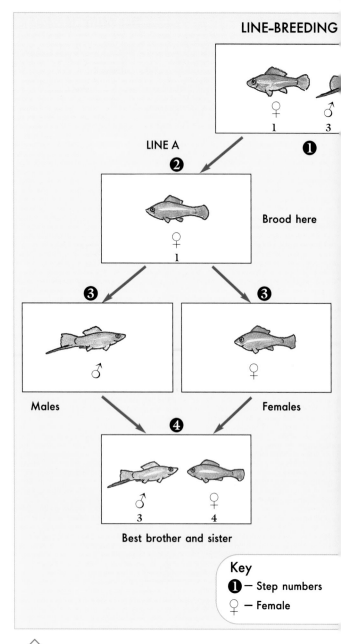

LINE A

Brood here

Males

Females

Best brother and sister

Key
- ❶ – Step numbers
- ♀ – Female

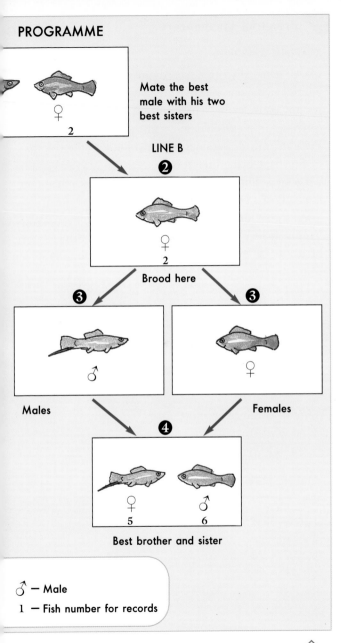

Mate the best male with his two best sisters

LINE B

② ♀ 2

Brood here

③ ♂

Males

③ ♀

Females

④ ♀ 5   ♂ 6

Best brother and sister

♂ — Male
1 — Fish number for records

KEEPING RECORDS

Good, detailed written records are essential to maintain control over your selective breeding methods when run for any considerable length of time. Without some kind of record, it is possible, in a short period of time, that these man-made varieties of fish could lose the colours or fin shape being bred for.

Using a simple card system, it is possible to maintain a record of a breeding project and therefore have a good source of reference to compile a 'pedigree', or 'family history' of a certain fish. Of course, this can also be placed on to the home computer, with photographs of the fish.

Here is an example of a simple record card that relates to a particular fish. It can be adapted to suit any additional requirements, such as details of colours and fin shapes etc – see key opposite for details.

A BREEDING CARD
Fish no.1: male
Origin: commercial shop stock
Type: Red Wagtail Platy

Mating			Brood			
Mating no.	Mate	Date	Date of birth	No. of males	No. of females	Line no.
1	2 ♀	6/1/02	5/2/02	20	25	
2						
3						
4						
5						
6						
7						
8						

Keeping accurate records will ensure your breeding programme stays focused.

- Each fish used for breeding will have his or her individual card, and number.
- Use the standard biological symbols to indicate the males ♂ and females ♀. (They represent the lance and shield of Mars ♂ for the male, and the mirror of Venus ♀ for the female.)
- Each fish used for breeding will carry a number. The first pair used will be shown as ♂1 and ♀2.

BREEDING-CARD KEY
- Mate no.: indicates each time the fish is used for breeding.
- Mate: indicates the fish mated with, the identification number and sex.
- Date: indicates the date the pair of fish is put together.
- Date of birth: indicates the date the brood are produced.
- No. of males: indicates the number of males saved from the brood.
- No. of females: indicates the number of females saved from the brood.
- Line no.: if running two or more lines in a line-breeding programme, place the number of the line in this column.

CHAPTER 7

PRODUCING AND REARING FRY

There are many factors that affect the production and rearing of livebearer fry – all of them the responsibility of the fishkeeper.

PREMATURE BIRTH

All the females covered in this book produce eggs that are held internally until they hatch just before birth. If the females are placed under stress (such as being confined in small breeding traps), they can prematurely release embryos that are only partly developed. In fact, they have the appearance of eggs, often with the developing fish visible inside. When this happens, there is no chance of these premature embryos surviving. This problem can be prevented by not placing gravid females under stress. For example, do not attempt to catch them in a net when they are close to giving birth.

FOODS FOR FRY

Newborn livebearer fry are able to take live foods, such as brine shrimp nauplii and microworm, as soon as they are born. To attain the growth rate that will enable the young fish to be large enough for sexing at three to four weeks old, they need to be fed these foods at least three to four times a day.

Brine shrimp is a relatively small crustacean found generally under the biological name of *Artemia salina*.

Brine shrimp nauplii is an ideal first food for newborn livebearer fry. If you do not wish to hatch your own, it can be purchased from aquatic outlets.

Brine shrimp eggs, correctly known as cysts, can be purchased from fish retail outlets or by post from adverts in fishkeeping magazines. The cysts can be hatched to produce live brine shrimp nauplii that are fed to the fry. Brine shrimp is a very important source of live food for aquarium fishes.

Microworm (*Panarellus silusiae*) is a very tiny nematode roundworm that is less than 1 mm in length. It is this small size that makes it a very good live food for baby fish. The worms can easily be cultivated and will produce vast numbers of tiny worms in a relatively short time.

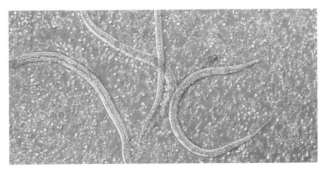

Microworm is also enjoyed by fry. Pictured: a close-up of the tiny worms.

Detailed culture methods of both these foods can be found in *Live Foods for Aquarium Fishes*, a title in this *Practical Fishkeeping* series.

As the fry grow, these live foods can be supplemented by special baby dry foods or crushed standard dry flake food.

CULLING

During a selective breeding programme, the fishkeeper has to plan ahead and be somewhat ruthless when it comes to keeping the young fish. This is achieved by culling out all the fish that are deformed or that show bent fins.

Culling is an on-going procedure that will start with the fry, and then move on to the young fish and even young adults that may display deformities as they develop.

Another factor that will require the use of culling is to raise only the number of fish that can be maintained in the size and number of tanks that the fishkeeper has. It is better to raise 50 good-quality fish than 200 runts.

Only the best-quality fry should be kept — the rest should be culled. Pictured: a healthy shoal of baby red swordtails, about 2 cm ($^3/_4$ in) in length.

Also note that at roughly 25-day intervals, a female livebearer can produce further broods. It is, of course, impossible to raise all of these fish, so it is imperative that the strict breeding methods are adhered to.

Any fish that are not required must be disposed of correctly. Healthy fish that do not carry a characteristic that you are breeding for, or those that you do not have space to house, can be offered to fishkeeping friends, or perhaps a local dealer who may want good, healthy fish.

The other option is euthanasia, something that must be considered if the fish are deformed. There are acceptable, humane methods, such as concussion, followed by destruction of the brain is best (e.g. blow to the head so the brain is instantly destroyed).

Full details of acceptable methods of euthanasia can be found in *Common Fish Ailments* in this *Practical Fishkeeping* series.

GROWING ON

When considering the numbers of fish that can be kept and grown on to adults, it is wise to use a standard for working out stocking densities. This will stop any overcrowding in the growing-on tanks, and it will be useful when only a limited number of tanks are available.

When calculating the number of fish a tank can hold, allow for the potential size the fish may reach. The rule gives the total length of fish (excluding the tails) that a tank can hold.

The rule is to multiply the length of the tank by the width in inches and divide this result by 12. This will give the total length of fish the tank can support. For example, a tank 24 in x 12 in x 12 in could hold 24 in of fish (60 cm x 30 cm x 30 cm = 60 cm of fish).

This means it could be 24 fish at 1 in (2.5 cm), 12 fish at 2 in (5 cm) or 6 fish at 4 in (10 cm) and so on. Note that these stocking levels can be increased somewhat if the tank is well filtered and maintained.

SEXING FISH

It is imperative that the sexes are separated at an early age and are then kept separate until they are required for breeding. It is possible to see signs of the sexes at three to four weeks old. These signs are the thickening of the anal fin on the males, which is the start of the gonopodium forming.

Sexing adult fish is considerably easier than identifying sex characteristics in immature, younger fry.
Pictured: adult female *X. variatus*: note the rounder body that is lacking in males of the same species.

Another early indication of having females in a brood is the starting of a dark area in the belly region just to the front of the anal fin. This dark area is known as the 'gravid spot'.

This procedure of separation ensures that the young fish do not mate, which is possible as soon as they can be sexed.

Random, uncontrolled matings will only lead to the ad-hoc breeding methods mentioned earlier in the book and an ensuing loss of control over any breeding programme.

GUPPIES

The guppy can cause the most problems in a selective breeding project. The main area of difficulty is obtaining the initial breeding stock. If breeding stock are fish that have been imported from the Far East, then the problem of obtaining a matched pair can be difficult.

The problem is that, while the males are usually sent in their individual colour varieties, the females arrive as a mixed group. This means that there can be all types of coloured females in one tank.

With careful observation, females could be selected to match the males. If the breeding stock is obtained this way, it is still possible to produce good-quality fish. It will, however, involve more work through in-breeding or line-breeding to establish a so-called 'pure line'. See also Chapter Six.

It is far easier if the stock can be obtained from a fishkeeping friend or a local breeder who keeps control of their breeding stock, and where the fish are from a direct line that has been selectively bred.

Most male lyretail varieties are incapable of breeding because of their very large gonopodiums. Pictured: a male tuxedo hifin lyretail swordtail.

SWORDTAILS

The swordtail (like the platy and molly) is not usually found in shops with males and females separated. So it is possible to obtain a pair of red swordtails from the same tank and to have a better chance that the fish are related.

There is still a chance that, because the exact family history of the fish is not known, the first brood produced by the fish could have some fish that are not red. This is when the process of culling and selection is necessary to start establishing the colour or shape of the fish required.

When working with the lyretail varieties of swordtails, that have long extensions on all the fins including the anal fin, most of the males are incapable of breeding. This is because they are unable to use their grossly enlarged gonopodium.

These fish are therefore bred by using a male with normal finnage and mating him to a lyretailed female of the same colour variety. Another way is to use sons that have not developed the lyretail characteristics and back-cross them with their mother.

Another point worth noting when breeding swordtails is that the best males are obtained from fish that do not start to obtain their swordtail caudal extensions until they are 6 cm (2.5 in) in length.

PLATIES

When breeding varieties of the platy *Xiphophorus variatus,* the growth rate is rather slow compared to the varieties of the platy *Xiphophorus maculatus*. It could be nine months before the full, striking colours of *X.variatus* are seen to their full advantage. See also page 15.

MOLLIES

When breeding the larger sailfin varieties of molly that can grow to 15 cm (6 in), tank sizes must be considered. A 91 cm (36 in) tank will hold 35 young fish for the first four weeks; after this, they should be moved to a larger tank of a minimum size of 122 cm (48 in).

Be careful if there is a need to move gravid female mollies to another tank, as netting and moving fish may result in premature birth. See also page 17.

OTHER LIVEBEARERS

There are many other true species of livebearing fish that are diverse in shape and size. However, compared to the large number of species, only a small percentage of them can be found in aquarium retail outlets.

There are very keen specialist fishkeepers who keep

There is a huge range of livebearing fish available to the hobby.
Pictured: *Poecilia sphenops* (above) and *Poecilia vivipara* (below).

and breed some of these rare species, and there are
livebearing fish societies (contacts for these
organisations can be found in *Practical Fishkeeping*
magazine).

CONCLUSION

This book by no means covers all the points of how to
breed these fascinating fish. What it hopefully does is
supply a commonsense approach to a very complicated
subject. It may encourage the reader to move on from
ad-hoc breeding methods and progress to establishing a
line of true breeding fish. Good luck!

DID YOU KNOW?

- Practical Fishkeeping is Britain's best-selling fishkeeping magazine.
- Practical Fishkeeping is published four weekly.
- It covers every area of the hobby for every fishkeeper from newcomer to expert.
- It covers tropical freshwater fish from community species to the rare and unusual and marine tropical fish and inverts.
- We look at ponds of all shapes and sizes from goldfish to Koi - coldwater aquarium fish.
- We publish hard-edged, in depth, up to date reviews of all the equipment you need to run a successful aquarium or pond.
- If you want to know more about the great hobby of fishkeeping it's exactly what you need.

Practical Fishkeeping
Introductory subscription offer

To subscribe to Practical Fishkeeping magazine, simply call

0845 601 1356

and quote FB11/A67 to receive 6 issues at a special price. Offer only open to UK residents.
For details of overseas rates, please call **+44 (0)1858 468811.**

**Practical Fishkeeping, Bretton Court, Bretton, Peterborough PE3 8DZ, Great Britain
Tel: 01733 282764**